The Playful Way to Knowing Yourself

Books by Roberta Allen

Nonfiction

Amazon Dream

Fast Fiction

The Playful Way to Serious Writing

The Playful Way to Knowing Yourself

Fiction

The Traveling Woman

The Daughter

Certain People

The Dreaming Girl

The Playful Way to Knowing Yourself

A Creative Workbook to Inspire Self-Discovery

Roberta Allen

Houghton Mifflin Company   Boston   New York   2003

For information about permission to reproduce selections
from this book, write to Permissions, Houghton Mifflin Company,
215 Park Avenue South, New York, New York 10003.

Visit our Web site: www.houghtonmifflinbooks.com.

Library of Congress Cataloging-in-Publication Data
    Allen, Roberta, date.
    The playful way to knowing yourself : a creative workbook
to inspire self-discovery / Roberta Allen.
        p. cm.
    ISBN 0-618-26924-X
    1. Self-perception—Problems, exercises, etc. I. Title.
    BF697.5.S43A44 2003
    158.1—dc21   2002191293

Printed in the United States of America

RRD 10 9 8 7 6 5 4 3 2 1

This book is for everyone who is searching

The Playful Way to Knowing Yourself

One day as I walked along a beautiful beach under a bright blue sky, I glanced at a woman in a chaise longue— a tourist like myself—and wondered, when she looked at the sky, if we saw the same blue. Was the shade she saw determined by the margarita she was drinking or by an argument she had had with her husband? Was the blue I saw determined by the elation I felt over giving myself this vacation?

Who was I here on this tropical isle? Was I the writer who had just finished a book? Was I the artist who drew pictures and took photographs? Who was I with my boyfriend? My family? My friends? My colleagues? My students? There are so many different parts of me, I mused. Are some parts more real than others?

The day I was thinking these thoughts I could have chosen to explore more of the island. But, instead, I sat in a chair by my cottage on the beach and opened a sketchbook I had brought just in case I felt the impulse to write or draw. I began jotting down ideas that became the basis for this book.

As an artist, I've always been interested in how we see ourselves and the world. I've always been interested in breaking down barriers of rational thinking so we may see beyond our usual limits, beyond the demands of our everyday lives, into our spirit, our soul.

Our views of ourselves are limited by our experience and by what we've been taught. My aim here is to redirect your focus instantly so you see yourself and the world in ways that not only ring true, but surprise you.

As a writer, I've always been impressed by the power of words: how writing things down helps us find what is true. As a teacher, I've seen how a single word, such as "envy" or "leaf," triggers a different response when each student is asked to write about it.

Sometimes when I see my students writing with great intensity, I am reminded of the faces I drew with that same intensity when I was a child. Those faces were my companions, my friends. They kept me company in my loneliest hours. Since I was not allowed by my mother and grandmother to play or get dirty, all my pent-up energy—my "aliveness"—went into my drawing.

I put so much pressure on the pencil when I drew that I deformed my middle finger. But that still seems to me a small price to pay. Years later, I would realize that pressure brings energy to the surface. Years later, I would call that "aliveness" energy.

I remember how afraid I was the day before I left on my journey alone to the Peruvian Amazon, and how alive I felt when, two days later, I walked the streets of Iquitos, Peru's largest Amazonian town. All my senses felt heightened. The hot, sweet-smelling air made me feel as though I were in a greenhouse.

I felt present, connected. I saw myself and the world from a state of "aliveness," in which I was no longer separate and alone but part of something much greater than myself.

I did not realize until later the tremendous energy that had been locked inside my fear. Living my childhood dream of going to the Amazon (where I could play and get dirty) allowed me to release that energy and let the "aliveness" out.

Though each one of us is unique, I believe we are all connected. We are all part of a much larger picture. What we see is a very small part. This book is my attempt to help you see more of yourself and others.

There are no right or wrong answers to the exercises in this book. There are only _your_ answers. Your answers are unique to you. No one else sees life exactly the way you see it.

This book offers a unique approach that allows you to see yourself from angles and perspectives you would not otherwise see. All you need to do is be open-minded, curious, and willing to respond instantly and imaginatively to exercises that invite you to explore your memories and beliefs, your desires and dreams, your secrets and fears, and how you relate to others.

The process is simple, easy, and fun. At the very least, you will get surprising glimpses of yourself. At best, you will have deep insights that lead you to action or to accepting yourself just as you are.

Do the exercises quickly and spontaneously. If you are someone who tends to pause and think, use a timer. As soon as you read the question and look at the picture, set it for two, three, or four minutes and go! The time limit you choose will depend upon the amount of space provided and how fast you write. Experiment to find out. By using this method, you bypass the judge inside you who might censor your response.

When you do each exercise, notice whether or not it has _energy_ for you; notice whether or not it makes you feel more alive. Energy is the spark that ignites when you connect with a place, a creature, a work of art, a sunset, a symphony, another human being. Energy is the invisible force behind the words. That invisible force is often locked inside a shell of fear and bursts forth when you break that shell.

An exercise with energy makes you feel something—even if it is just for a moment. The feeling may be faint or intense: you may feel sad or happy, excited or distressed. Feeling more alive is not always feeling good. Give yourself permission to feel whatever comes up. Your emotions are part of you and part of this process.

You know you've tapped something important in yourself when your exercise has a lot of energy. In order for that to happen, allow yourself to write whatever comes to mind, no matter how silly it may sound to you, how nonsensical, foolish, or even scary! Follow your energy wherever it leads you. Allow yourself to be who you are.

Be brief. Use the space provided for each exercise. Get to the heart of what you're saying as soon as you can. This will keep you from writing endlessly, straying off course, and losing your initial energy. Your exercises should be the verbal equivalent of quick artist sketches, in which a model is captured with just a few strokes.

As you go through this book, you will have opportunities to pause and reflect on previous exercises and to continue the ones that are most charged or that feel incomplete. Keep a notebook handy for this purpose.

Not every exercise will have energy for you. When you draw a blank on one exercise, go on to the next. If you find yourself resisting an exercise, come back to it later. Do the ones that come easily.

Years ago I had a masseur who started each session with the words "It's not serious." As he worked on my tense back, relaxing all the muscles, he continued saying "It's not serious" till it became a kind of chant. Eventually my back problems disappeared, but the words "It's not serious" stayed in my mind.

The things that made me so tense seem laughable now. At the time, I was the freelance art director of a French food company, overwhelmed by deadlines.

Joel, my masseur, was right. It wasn't serious. Remember those words when doing the exercises in this book.

The loosening-up exercises that begin each of the four sections are intended to get you going. Read each question and quickly write whatever comes to mind.

Loosening-up exercise

If you were asked to choose seven words to describe yourself, what would they be?

1. _____

2. _____

3. _____

4. _____

5. _____

6. _____

7. _____

Loosening-up exercise

If you were asked to choose seven objects that have meaning for you, what objects would you choose?

1. _____

2. _____

3. _____

4. _____

5. _____

6. _____

7. _____

If you were asked to choose seven colors that have meaning for you, what colors would you choose?

1. _____

2. _____

3. _____

4. _____

5. _____

6. _____

7. _____

Loosening-up exercise

If you were asked to choose seven places that have meaning for you, what places would you choose?

1. _____

2. _____

3. _____

4. _____

5. _____

6. _____

7. _____

Imagine looking in this mirror. What do you see about yourself that you like? What do you see that you dislike?

_____

_____

_____

_____

_____

_____

_____

_____

_____

_____

_____

_____

What keeps you balanced?

_____

_____

_____

_____

_____

_____

_____

_____

_____

_____

_____

_____

What keeps you from being still?

_____

_____

_____

_____

_____

_____

_____

_____

_____

_____

_____

What relaxes you?

_____

_____

_____

_____

_____

_____

_____

_____

_____

_____

_____

_____

What gives you pleasure?

_____

_____

_____

_____

_____

_____

_____

_____

_____

_____

_____

_____

What is holding you back?

_____

_____

_____

_____

_____

_____

_____

_____

_____

_____

_____

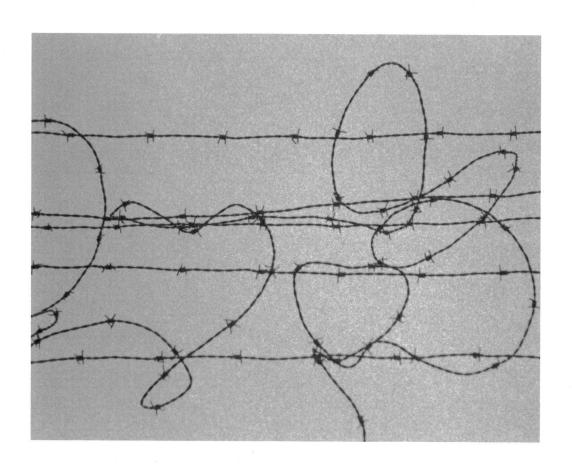

What makes you different?

_____

_____

_____

_____

_____

_____

_____

_____

_____

_____

_____

_____

What makes you shine?

_____

_____

_____

_____

_____

_____

_____

_____

_____

_____

_____

45

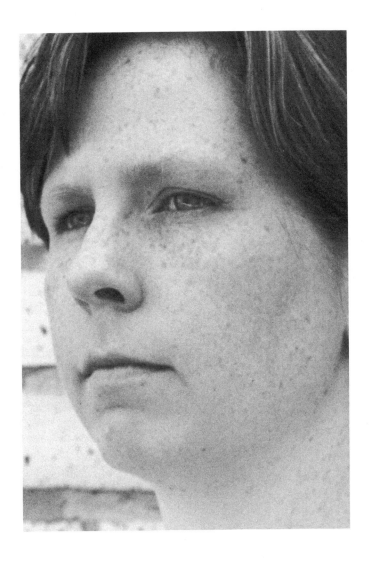

Imagine wanting to impress this woman. What would you say about yourself?

_____

_____

_____

_____

_____

_____

_____

_____

_____

_____

_____

What is your idea of perfection?

_____

_____

_____

_____

_____

_____

_____

_____

_____

_____

_____

_____

What is she hearing about you?

_____

_____

_____

_____

_____

_____

_____

_____

_____

_____

_____

What fascinates you?

_____

_____

_____

_____

_____

_____

_____

_____

_____

_____

_____

_____

_____

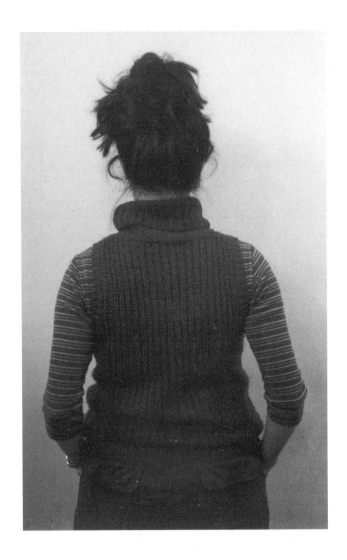

54

Who or what is she looking at that's more important than you?

_____

_____

_____

_____

_____

_____

_____

_____

_____

_____

What can you do to simplify your life?

_____

_____

_____

_____

_____

_____

_____

_____

_____

_____

_____

Imagine finding this figure drawn in the sand. Is it a circle? A zero? The letter "O"? Relate this figure to your life.

_____

_____

_____

_____

_____

_____

_____

_____

_____

_____

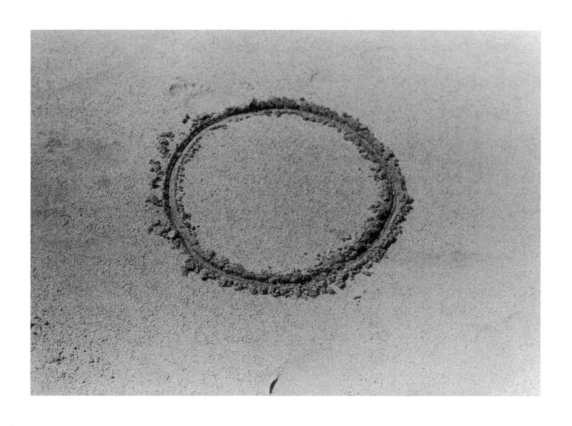

Imagine finding the number "2" drawn in the sand. What comes to mind when you look at this figure?

_____

_____

_____

_____

_____

_____

_____

_____

_____

_____

61

What makes you feel loved?

_____

_____

_____

_____

_____

_____

_____

_____

_____

_____

_____

_____

What risks have you taken?

_____

_____

_____

_____

_____

_____

_____

_____

_____

_____

_____

_____

_____

What challenges lie ahead?

_____

_____

_____

_____

_____

_____

_____

_____

_____

_____

_____

Imagine yourself here watching a beautiful sunset. What are you grateful for?

_____

_____

_____

_____

_____

What are you grateful for in the place where you are right now?

_____

_____

_____

_____

_____

If she could foresee one accomplishment in your future, what would you like it to be?

_____

_____

_____

_____

_____

_____

_____

_____

_____

_____

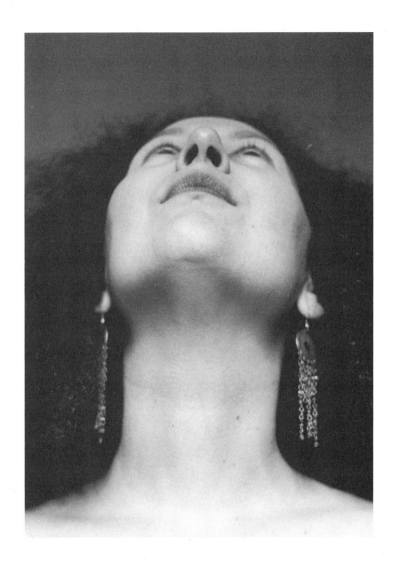

Review #1

Take time now to go back and look over the exercises you've done. Use your notebook to answer the next three questions:

1. Which of your answers surprise you? Why?

2. Is there any one exercise that feels more charged than the others? See where that energy takes you when you continue. Stop as soon as the energy runs out.

3. Are there any other exercises that feel charged? Are there exercises that feel incomplete? Go with your energy. Complete those exercises now. You know an exercise is finished when your energy is spent and the exercise _feels_ complete.

What insights about yourself have come to light?

_____

_____

_____

_____

_____

_____

_____

_____

_____

_____

_____

_____

Loosening-up exercise

What words would you use to describe your mother?

1. _____

2. _____

3. _____

4. _____

5. _____

6. _____

7. _____

Loosening-up exercise

What words would you use to describe your father?

1. _____

2. _____

3. _____

4. _____

5. _____

6. _____

7. _____

What words would your mother use to describe you?

1. _____

2. _____

3. _____

4. _____

5. _____

6. _____

7. _____

Loosening-up exercise

What words would your father use to describe you?

1. _____

2. _____

3. _____

4. _____

5. _____

6. _____

7. _____

Imagine someone important to you sitting in this chair.
What would you say to this person that you've never
said before?

_____

_____

_____

_____

_____

_____

_____

_____

_____

What emotional storms have you weathered?

_____

_____

_____

_____

_____

_____

_____

_____

_____

_____

_____

If you could, what parts of yourself would you throw out?

_____

_____

_____

_____

_____

_____

_____

_____

_____

_____

_____

Imagine three people who know you well sitting in these chairs and discussing your problems. Who are they and what are they saying?

_____

_____

_____

_____

_____

_____

_____

_____

_____

_____

What is it about you that is making this person anxious?

_____

_____

_____

_____

_____

_____

_____

_____

_____

_____

_____

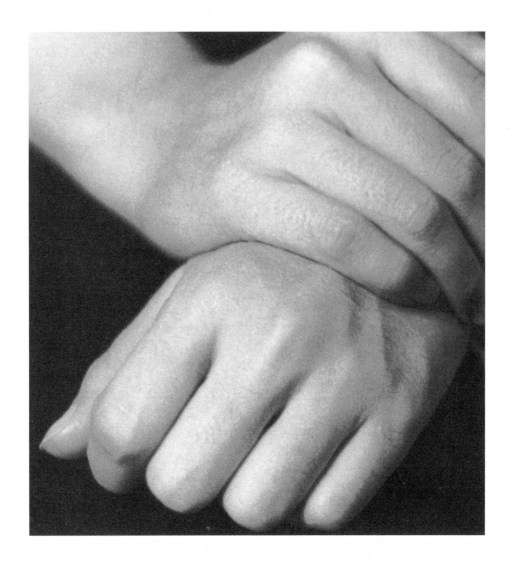

What have you done that no one knows about?

What roles come to mind when you look at this man? Do you play the same roles? Does someone close to you?

_____

_____

_____

_____

_____

_____

_____

_____

_____

_____

_____

What are you afraid of exposing about yourself?

_____

_____

_____

_____

_____

_____

_____

_____

_____

_____

_____

Imagine this woman seeing you exactly the way you want to be seen. What does she see?

_____

_____

_____

_____

_____

_____

_____

_____

_____

_____

_____

What part of you is locked inside this house?

_____

_____

_____

_____

_____

What can you do to free that part of yourself?

_____

_____

_____

_____

_____

What door have you closed?

_____

_____

_____

_____

_____

_____

_____

_____

_____

_____

_____

_____

What have you left undone?

_____

_____

_____

_____

_____

_____

_____

_____

_____

_____

_____

_____

What makes you feel vulnerable?

_____

_____

_____

_____

_____

_____

_____

_____

_____

_____

_____

_____

What does she know about you that no one else knows?

_____

_____

_____

_____

_____

_____

_____

_____

_____

_____

_____

_____

What could these boys teach you? What could you teach them?

_____

_____

_____

_____

_____

_____

_____

_____

_____

_____

_____

What message just for you is hidden in this ancient writing?

_____

_____

_____

_____

_____

_____

_____

_____

_____

_____

_____

Review #2

Take time now to go back and look over the exercises you've done. Use your notebook to answer the next three questions:

1. Which of your answers surprise you? Why?

2. Is there any one exercise that feels more charged than the others? See where that energy takes you when you continue. Stop as soon as the energy runs out.

3. Are there any other exercises that feel charged? Are there exercises that feel incomplete? Go with your energy. Complete those exercises now. You know an exercise is finished when your energy is spent and the exercise _feels_ complete.

What insights about yourself have come to light?

_____

_____

_____

_____

_____

_____

_____

_____

_____

_____

_____

Loosening-up exercise

What words would you use to describe your spouse, partner, or best friend?

1. _____

2. _____

3. _____

4. _____

5. _____

6. _____

7. _____

What words would you use to describe your enemies?

1. _____

2. _____

3. _____

4. _____

5. _____

6. _____

7. _____

Loosening-up exercise

What words would your spouse, partner, or best friend use to describe you?

1. _____

2. _____

3. _____

4. _____

5. _____

6. _____

7. _____

Loosening-up exercise

What words would your enemies use to describe you?

    1. _____

    2. _____

    3. _____

    4. _____

    5. _____

    6. _____

    7. _____

What are you holding on to from the past?

_____

_____

_____

_____

_____

_____

_____

_____

_____

_____

_____

Do you see something of yourself in this little girl? If so, what?

_____

_____

_____

_____

_____

_____

_____

_____

_____

_____

_____

What makes life magical?

_____

_____

_____

_____

_____

_____

_____

_____

_____

_____

_____

_____

If you were to give this baby something you lacked early in life, what would it be?

_____

_____

_____

_____

_____

_____

_____

_____

_____

_____

_____

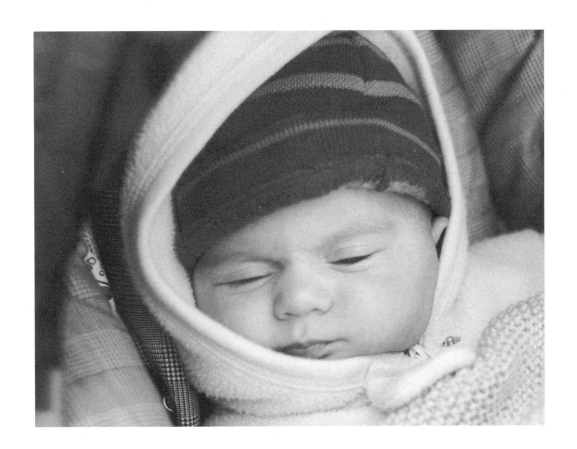

If you were to tell this boy what you value most in life,
what would you say?

_____

_____

_____

_____

_____

_____

_____

_____

_____

_____

_____

What could this man say or do to make you angry?

_____

_____

_____

_____

_____

What could this man say or do to make you happy?

_____

_____

_____

_____

_____

What would make you feel the way this woman feels?

_____

_____

_____

_____

_____

_____

_____

_____

_____

_____

_____

What makes life juicy?

_____

_____

_____

_____

_____

_____

_____

_____

_____

_____

_____

What do you hunger for?

_____

_____

_____

_____

_____

_____

_____

_____

_____

_____

_____

Imagine telling your deepest secrets to the person behind this door. What are you saying?

_____

_____

_____

_____

_____

_____

_____

_____

_____

_____

_____

If you were superstitious, and this black cat crossed your path, what would you be afraid might happen?

_____

_____

_____

_____

_____

_____

_____

_____

_____

_____

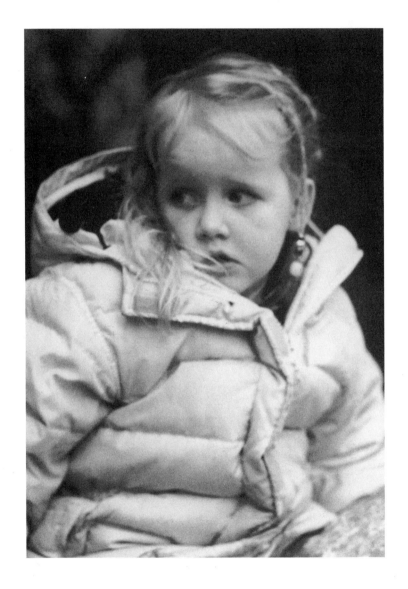

What fears do you have in common with this little girl? What fears have you overcome?

_____

_____

_____

_____

_____

_____

_____

_____

_____

_____

_____

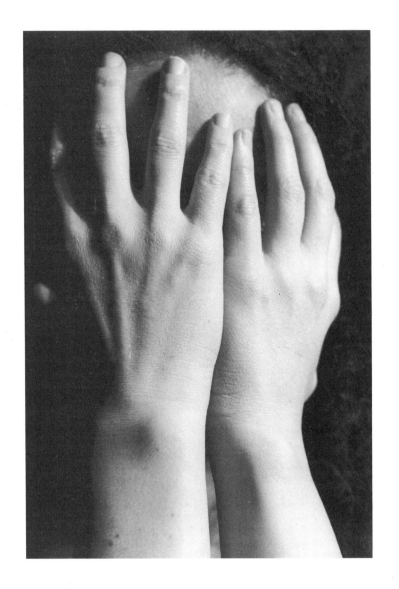

What game is she playing with you? What games do you play with others?

_____

_____

_____

_____

_____

_____

_____

_____

_____

_____

What is behind this door that you want?

_____

_____

_____

_____

Imagine having the key. What is stopping you from opening the door?

_____

_____

_____

_____

_____

147

If you could go anywhere you wanted right now, where would you go?

_____

_____

_____

_____

_____

_____

_____

_____

_____

_____

What makes you feel lonely?

_____

_____

_____

_____

_____

_____

_____

_____

_____

_____

_____

Imagine this man telling you something important, something you need to hear. What is he saying?

_____

_____

_____

_____

_____

_____

_____

_____

_____

_____

_____

Imagine something wonderful happening to you in this house. What is it?

_____

_____

_____

_____

_____

_____

_____

_____

_____

_____

_____

Review #3

Take time now to go back and look over the exercises you've done. Use your notebook to answer the next three questions:

1. Which of your answers surprise you? Why?

2. Is there any one exercise that feels more charged than the others? See where that energy takes you when you continue. Stop as soon as the energy runs out.

3. Are there any other exercises that feel charged? Are there exercises that feel incomplete? Go with your energy. Complete those exercises now. You know an exercise is finished when your energy is spent and the exercise _feels_ complete.

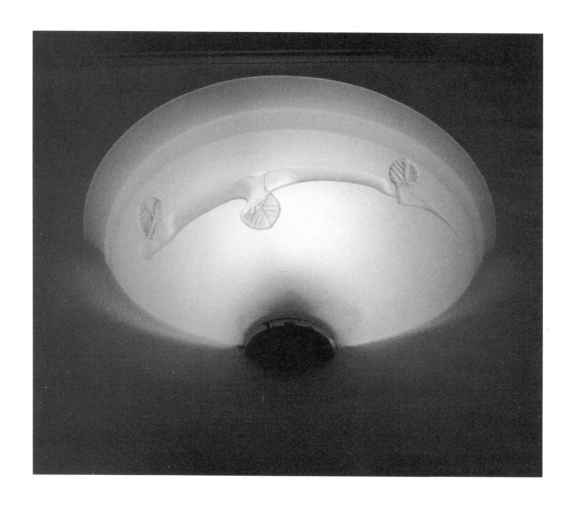

What insights about yourself have come to light?

_____

_____

_____

_____

_____

_____

_____

_____

_____

_____

_____

Loosening-up exercise

What feelings describe you?

1. _____

2. _____

3. _____

4. _____

5. _____

6. _____

7. _____

Loosening-up exercise

What habits describe you?

1. _____

2. _____

3. _____

4. _____

5. _____

6. _____

7. _____

Loosening-up exercise

What beliefs describe you?

1. _____

2. _____

3. _____

4. _____

5. _____

6. _____

7. _____

Loosening-up exercise

What else describes you?

1. _____

2. _____

3. _____

4. _____

5. _____

6. _____

7. _____

If you were lost, what would help you find your way?

_____

_____

_____

_____

_____

_____

_____

_____

_____

_____

_____

What makes you a survivor?

_____

_____

_____

_____

_____

_____

_____

_____

_____

_____

_____

_____

_____

What keeps you going?

_____

_____

_____

_____

_____

_____

_____

_____

_____

_____

_____

_____

What other worlds entice you?

_____

_____

_____

_____

_____

_____

_____

_____

_____

_____

_____

What divides you?

_____

_____

_____

_____

_____

_____

_____

_____

_____

_____

_____

_____

What makes you feel whole?

_____

_____

_____

_____

_____

_____

_____

_____

_____

_____

_____

_____

If you were to give her one piece of advice about life, what would you say?

_____

_____

_____

_____

_____

_____

_____

_____

_____

_____

What inspires you?

_____

_____

_____

_____

_____

_____

_____

_____

_____

_____

_____

_____

What makes you feel small?

_____

_____

_____

_____

_____

_____

_____

_____

_____

_____

_____

_____

Whom do you look down upon?

_____

_____

_____

_____

_____

_____

_____

_____

_____

_____

_____

_____

What don't you understand?

_____

_____

_____

_____

_____

_____

_____

_____

_____

_____

_____

What is left when you take everything away?

_____

_____

_____

_____

_____

_____

_____

_____

_____

_____

_____

_____

What do you hold sacred?

_____

_____

_____

_____

_____

_____

_____

_____

_____

_____

_____

_____

Imagine this man giving you sound advice. What is he saying?

_____

_____

_____

_____

_____

_____

_____

_____

_____

_____

Imagine yourself floating among these clouds in harmony with everyone and everything. What can you do to make that happen?

_____

_____

_____

_____

_____

_____

_____

_____

_____

_____

Where are you going? Where would you like to be in five years?

_____

_____

_____

_____

_____

_____

_____

_____

_____

_____

What mysteries have you glimpsed?

_____

_____

_____

_____

_____

_____

_____

_____

_____

_____

_____

What would you like to leave behind?

_____

_____

_____

_____

_____

_____

_____

_____

_____

_____

_____

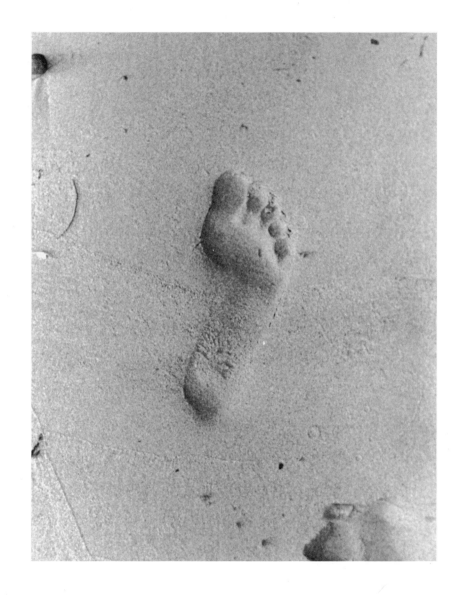

199

Review #4

Take time now to go back and look over the exercises you've done. Use your notebook to answer the next three questions:

1. Which of your answers surprise you? Why?

2. Is there any one exercise that feels more charged than the others? See where that energy takes you when you continue. Stop as soon as the energy runs out.

3. Are there any other exercises that feel charged? Are there exercises that feel incomplete? Go with your energy. Complete those exercises now. You know an exercise is finished when your energy is spent and the exercise _feels_ complete.

What insights about yourself have come to light?

_____

_____

_____

_____

_____

_____

_____

_____

_____

_____

_____

You have come to the end of the book, but you haven't come to the end of this process. Now is the time to consider how to use what you've learned about yourself. Read the following questions. Use your notebook to respond.

1. Who might benefit from what you have discovered?

2. What actions might you take now that you wouldn't have taken before?

3. What can you now accept about yourself?

4. What else would you like to know about yourself?

5. Now that you've tapped into your energy, can you think of ways to tap into it more often? Are there thoughts, such as "It's not serious," or images from this book or your own imagination, that you can focus your attention on, to help you feel more alive?

Just because you've done the exercises once doesn't mean you can't go back and start all over again. The same exercises will elicit different responses at different times—all of which may be true.

Your responses may change with your moods, with the weather, with the seasons, with time. As the Greek philosopher Heraclitus once said, You can't step in the same river twice.

If you would like more information about the Playful Way method or my workshops, seminars, and creativity coaching, please e-mail me at Robertaallen7@aol.com. You can also visit my Web sites:

http://hometown.aol.com/Roall

www.playfulway.com

Acknowledgments

Many thanks to my editor, Susan Canavan, for her support. A special thanks to Lorrie Bodger for her generosity and advice. Joel Agee once again offered valuable suggestions. Thanks also to my agent, DeAnna Heindel. And last but not least, Craig.

JERRY BAUER

Roberta Allen is a creativity coach and the author of <u>The Playful Way to Serious Writing</u> and <u>Fast Fiction: Creating Fiction in Five Minutes</u>. She has also written two collections of stories, <u>The Traveling Woman</u> and <u>Certain People</u>; a novella in stories, <u>The Daughter</u>; a novel, <u>The Dreaming Girl</u>; and a travel memoir, <u>Amazon Dream</u>. Allen is on the faculty of the New School University and has taught in the writing program at Columbia University and in numerous private workshops. She is also a visual artist who has exhibited worldwide, with work in the collection of the Metropolitan Museum of Art and Bibliothèque du France, Paris. She lives in New York City.